Juicing for Weight Loss

101 Delicious Juicing Recipes That Help You
Lose Weight Naturally Fast, Increase Energy
and Feel Great

Table of Contents

Introduction

Thank you for purchasing the book, *Juicing for Weight Loss: Delicious Juicing Recipes That Help You Lose Weight Naturally Fast, Increase Energy and Feel Great.*

We are thrilled to invite you to a life-altering journey, during which you will discover the true benefits that Mother Nature can offer us.

Getting yourself this amazing collection of juicing recipes will be your first step to an exciting way of providing yourself with a full-scale of vitamins, minerals, nutrients, and other microelements and shedding all your excess weight like you never had it.

Let us explain how it works with the help of juicing. In fact, juicing is no miracle, magic, or professional cooking trick. It can simply be defined as the process of extracting or squeezing the juice from whole vegetables and fruit. We cannot deny that it has become a modern buzzword, but do you think it is easy to attract the crowd's attention for no special reason? You know that it is not. So, the reason why so many people have heartily embarked on juicing is because of the numerous benefits that it provides.

The benefits of juicing

The first and probably most essential benefit is weight loss. Juicing is sure to help you in the tough process of fighting your pounds, as by taking your calories with juice, rich in nutrients, you will boost your metabolism, provide yourself with energy and avoid stuffing your stomach with empty calories. Indeed, liquid is easier to be absorbed in our body than solid food, and though munching our veggies is not at all bad, drinking them is more enjoyable, plus it gives our digestive tract a chance to rest from handling the hard fiber.

Another good reason to opt for juicing is to keep away from carton juices, which are loaded with sugar, preservatives, colorants, odorants, and other chemicals. Thus, juicing is the best way of saving your body from intoxication by supplying it with a myriad of vitamins and phytonutrients that are present in fresh, organic fruits and vegetables.

Another benefit that is worth mentioning is the ultimate detoxification that is easy to achieve through juicing. Whole plants contain insoluble fiber, which is hard to be absorbed, so therefore taking your vegetables and fruits in a liquid form provides you with important digestive enzymes, which are usually locked away in whole plants. By adopting the habit of juicing, you pave your way to healthier eating patterns, because after a glass of freshly squeezed orange juice, you will hardly want to spoil your diet with junk food. After experiencing this fresh splash of vitamins, you will integrate juicing into your daily life by making it one of your best kitchen habits.

And finally, you will find some ease at persuading your kids to eat their veggies. Moreover, they will start asking for them…

The mentioned reasons are just the tip of the iceberg. In fact, juicing can become the key factor for your healthy lifestyle. Never again you will experience such annoying things like fatigue, sickness, inflation, constipation, acne, etc. How come? The answer is so simple. Juicing allows for consumption the of plenty of vitamins in a matter of minutes, while munching through two carrots, a handful of strawberries, kale, broccoli, spinach, and Brussels sprouts might take weeks.

The benefits of juicing are obvious. But is it as simple as placing all the content of your fridge in a juicer and squeezing the juice out of it? Certainly not. There are a few things one should consider before starting this exciting activity and among the first things is moderation. As mentioned, juicing allows for momentary consumption of an arsenal of vitamins and thus a decent number of calories, so make sure you do not put the stress of fruits, rich in carbs, to provoke leaps of insulin levels. To not break your head with calculations, it is easier to get yourself a recipe book and follow the ingredient list as close as you can. Basing yourself on a healthy juicing cookbook, rather than the content of your fridge, will help you make best use of green leafy plants, citrus fruits, vegetables, rich in proteins, soluble fiber, and sulfur. Secondly, do not rip your budget buying imported, exotic and out of season fruits and vegetables. This strikes not only the wallet but also the stomach. Local, organic and in season whole plants are a lot cheaper and, at the same, time a lot healthier.

And, finally, be active. If you are about to drink a glass of banana and strawberry juice, then you will have to work it out so that the vitamins are in, and calories are out. So, it is important to keep in mind your caloric intake and make sure you waste the received calories in your daily activities or in sport.

We hope you have already got yourself a juicer and are picking the recipe that caught your attention first, as you are about to make your first glass of freshly squeezed juice.

<u>Chapter One: The Best Fruit and Veggie Juice Recipes</u>

Beet Carrot Apple Juice

Serves 2

Ingredients:

- 5 carrots, chopped
- 1 small beet, chopped
- 1 apple, cored and chopped
- ¼ cup fresh mint sprigs

Directions:

1. Wash the carrots, apple, beet, and mint and pass through a juicer.
2. Pour the juice into a glass, give a stir, and enjoy.

Veggie Detox Juice

Serves 1

Ingredients:

- 2 garlic cloves
- 3 medium carrots
- 1 medium beet
- 1 radish
- A handful of parsley

Directions:

1. Peel the beet, carrots, radish, and garlic and wash the parsley.
2. Run all ingredients through a juicer and drink immediately.
3. Great to drink 1-2 times a day.

Superpower Tropic Juice

Serves 2

Ingredients:

- 1 medium kiwi, peeled
- 1 medium ripe papaya, peeled, seeded, cut
- 1 small pineapple, peeled, cored, and sliced
- 1 (1-inch) piece fresh ginger, peeled
- ½ cup fresh young coconut water

Directions:

1. Peel and slice the papaya, pineapple, kiwi, and ginger. Process through a juicer.
2. Stir in the coconut water.
3. Pour the juice into glasses and enjoy.

Colorful Juice for Weight Loss

Serves 1

Ingredients:

- 1 orange
- ¼ fresh pineapple
- ½ handful cilantro
- ½ small jalapeno, seeded

Directions:

1. Peel the pineapple and orange and process through a juicer along with jalapeno and cilantro.
2. Pour the juice into a glass and enjoy.

Grapefruit Juice

Serves 1

Ingredients:
- 2 grapefruits, peeled
- 1 red bell pepper
- 2 pears
- 6 carrots

Directions:
1. Thoroughly wash the carrots, pears and grapefruits, peel and cut into chunks. Throw into a juicer along with red pepper.
2. Process and drink immediately.

Healthy Weight Loss Juice

Serves 1

Ingredients:
- 1 ruby grapefruit
- 1 orange
- 2 carrots
- ½ inch (1 cm) piece of ginger

Directions:
1. Wash and peel all ingredients.
2. Pass through a juicer and drink immediately.

Cabbage Orange Juice for Weight Loss

Serves 1

Ingredients:
- ½ young cabbage
- 1 small carrot
- 3 oranges, peeled
- ½ lemon juice
- a thumb size piece of ginger
- Ice cubes

Directions:
1. Run the carrot, ginger, cabbage, and oranges through a juicer.
2. Pour into a glass, add the lemon juice, stir well, and enjoy.

Carrot Cucumber Skinny Juice

Serves 1

Ingredients:

- 1 cucumber
- 3 carrots
- ½ or 1 lime

Directions:

1. Thoroughly wash the carrots, cucumber, and lime.
2. Run all ingredients through a juicer.
3. Pour the juice into a glass over ice and enjoy.

Slimming Apple Plum Juice Recipe

Serves 1

Ingredients:
- 3 plums
- ½ apple
- 1 cucumber
- ¼ lemon

Directions:
1. Wash the plums, apple, cucumber, and lemon. Add to a juicer and process.
2. Pour into a glass and enjoy immediately.

Fitness Juice Recipe

Serves 1

Ingredients:

- ½ cucumber
- 5 carrots, halved
- 1 apple, quartered
- ½ beet
- 1 rib celery

Directions:

1. Add the carrots, apple, cucumber, beet, and celery to a juicer and run until all ingredients are gone.
2. Pour the juice into a tall glass and enjoy immediately.

Energy Boosting Healthy Juice

Serves 1

Ingredients:

- 2 large carrots
- 1 apple
- Small handful of parsley
- 1 medium beetroot
- 1 stalk celery
- 1 inch of cucumber

Directions:

1. Thoroughly wash all the vegetables and apple under running water.
2. Peel the beetroot.
3. Run all the ingredients though a juicer along with parsley.
4. Pour into a glass over crushed ice.

Easy Juicing Recipe for Body Cleanse

Serves 1

Ingredients:
- ½ medium cucumber
- 1 smallish beet
- 2 red or green cabbage leaves
- 4 medium carrots

Directions:
1. Thoroughly wash the vegetables.
2. Cut the carrot ends and discard the greens.
3. Peel the beet and quarter it.
4. Pass all the ingredients through a juicer, pour into a glass and drink immediately.

Fat Burning Apple Carrot Juice with Celery

Serves 1

Ingredients:
- ½ cucumber
- 3 carrots
- 2 celery sticks
- 1 apple

Directions:
1. Thoroughly wash the carrots, cucumber, apple, and celery sticks.
2. Chop into chunks and run through a juicer.
3. Pour the juice into a glass and drink immediately.

Strawberry-Cucumber Juice

Serves 2

Ingredients:

- 1 large cucumber, peeled, cut into chunks
- 6 fresh strawberries, hulled
- 2 medium carrots, peeled
- 1 large red apple, quartered

Directions:

1. Wash the fruits and vegetables. Peel the cucumber and carrots.
2. Pass through a juicer along with strawberries and serve over ice cubes.

Apple Berry Juice

Serves 2

Ingredients:
- 3 apples, cored
- 1 cup cranberry juice
- 1 cup fresh blueberries

Directions:
1. Process the apples and blueberries through a juicer and pour into a pitcher.
2. Add the cranberry juice, stir well, and enjoy over ice.

Orange Pineapple Chili

Serves 1

Ingredients:
- ½ pineapple
- ½ lime, peeled
- 7 long carrots
- ½ small chili

Directions:
1. Remove the rind from the lime.
2. Trim the ends of carrots and discard the greens. Run through a juicer along with lime, pineapple, and chili.
3. Pour into a tall glass, add 2-3 cubes of ice and drink immediately.

Ginger Pear Celery Juice

Serves 1

Ingredients:
- 5 celery stalks
- 2 pears
- 1-inch piece of fresh ginger root

Directions:
1. Wash the pears and celery and cut into chunks. Pass through a juicer along with ginger.
2. Let sit for 2-5 minutes and enjoy.

Strawberry Tomato Juice

Serves 1-2

Ingredients:
- 3 ripe tomatoes, cut into quarters
- 2 cups strawberries
- 3 basil leaves

Directions:
1. Wash the strawberries, tomatoes and basil leaves and process through a juicer.
2. Pour into a glass over ice, garnish with a basil leave and serve.

Spicy Apple Lemonade

Serves 2

Ingredients:
- ½ lemon
- 3 apples, quartered
- 1 yellow pepper, cut into chunks
- 1-inch piece of ginger root

Directions:
1. Core the apples and cut into quarters. Remove the seeds from the pepper.
2. Add all the ingredients to a juicer and process.
3. Drink immediately.

Slimming Detox Drink

Serves 1

Ingredients:

- 5 celery stalks
- 5 long carrots
- ½ lemon, peeled
- 2 oranges, peeled
- 1 beetroot, greens removed
- 1 small handful of spinach
- 1-inch knob of ginger root

Directions:

1. Thoroughly wash all the ingredients. Peel the oranges and lemon and run through a juicer along with beetroot, celery, ginger, and spinach.
2. Pour into a tall glass and drink immediately.

Rich and Fulfilling Juice Recipe

Serves 1

Ingredients:
- ½ avocado
- 1 large carrot
- 1 orange
- 1 fresh or dried apricot

Directions:
1. Peel the carrot and orange and run through a juicer.
2. Pour the extracted juice into a blender, add the avocado and fresh or dried apricot and pulse until smooth.
3. Enjoy over ice.

The Best Veggie Juice Recipe for Weight Loss

Serves 1

Ingredients:
- 2 carrots
- 2 celery stalks
- 1 green apple
- 2 tomatoes
- 1 handful of parsley
- ½ of a beet
- 1 whole lemon (peeled)
- ½ inch knob of ginger

Directions:
1. Wash the carrots, apple, tomatoes and pass through a juicer along with celery, parsley, beet, lemon, and ginger.
2. Pour the juice into a tall glass and drink immediately.

Pumpkin Pie Juice

Serves 1

Ingredients:
- 3 carrots
- 1 small pumpkin, cut into cubes
- 1 apple (or pear)
- ½ inch ginger
- ¼ tsp of spices such as cinnamon, cloves or nutmeg

Directions:
1. Using a sharp knife peel the pumpkin, cut into cubes. Core the apple and run through a juicer along with carrots, ginger, and pumpkin.
2. Pour into a glass, stir in the spices and drink immediately.

Carrot Apple Ginger Juice

Serves 1-2

Ingredients:

- 5-6 carrots, peeled, ends trimmed
- 2 apples, cut into quarters
- ¼ teaspoon of cinnamon
- 1-inch piece of fresh ginger root, peeled

Directions:

1. Wash the apples and carrots and run through a juicer along with ginger.
2. Pour into a glass, stir in the cinnamon and drink immediately.

Grapefruit and Pineapple Juice for Weight Loss

Serves 1

Ingredients:
- 4 rounds of pineapple
- 1 grapefruit (juice of 1 grapefruit)
- 1 cup water

Directions:
1. Peel the pineapple and slice into rounds.
2. Run through a juicer along with the grapefruit. Pour the juice into a tall glass, add 1 cup water, stir well and drink immediately.

Apple Blackberry and Ginger Juice

Serves 1

Ingredients:

- 2-3 apples, quartered
- 1 cup blackberries
- ½-inch fresh ginger

Directions:

1. Peel the apples, cut into quarters, and pass through a juicer along with ginger and blackberries.
2. Pour the juice into a glass, stir well and drink immediately.

Avocado Mix for Weight Loss

Serves 1

Ingredients:
- ½ ripe avocado
- ½ small pineapple
- 2 apples, cored, quartered
- ½ stick celery
- 1 small handful of spinach leaves
- 1 small piece of peeled lime
- ½ of medium cucumber
- Ice cubes

Directions:
1. Core the apples and cut into quarters.
2. Run through a juicer along with the cucumber, lime, spinach, pineapple, and celery.
3. Peel the avocado and put in a blender. Add a couple of ice cubes and pulse for 20-30 seconds until smooth.
4. In a glass, combine the avocado mixture with the extracted juice, stir well and drink.

Hot Apple Juice

Serves 1

Ingredients:

- 3 apples
- A pinch of cinnamon

Directions:

1. Wash the apples, core, and cut into quarters.
2. Add to a juicer and juice. Pour the juice into a small pot and heat over low heat. Make sure not to boil.
3. Pour the hot juice into a cup, sprinkle with cinnamon and enjoy.

Lemon Ginger Juice

Serves 1

Ingredients:

- 2 carrots
- ½ inch of fresh ginger
- ½ lemon
- 2 apples
- 2 ice cubes

Directions:

1. Wash the lemon, carrots and apples and place in a juicer. Add the ginger and process.
2. Pour the juice in a tall glass over ice cubes and drink.

Citrus Watermelon Mint Juicing Recipe

Serves 1

Ingredients:

- 4 cups watermelon, cubed
- ½ lime
- ¼ orange
- ½ cucumber, unpeeled
- 4-5 sprigs of mint (or to taste)

Directions:

1. Peel the orange and lime and run through a juicer along with mint and cucumber.
2. Finally, juice the watermelon.
3. Pour the juice into a tall glass over ice, stir well, decorate with mint, and serve.

Pink Grapefruit Lime Juicing for Weight Loss Recipe

Serves 1

Ingredients:
- 2 pink grapefruits
- 1 lime

Directions:
1. Using a juicer or a citrus press, juice the grapefruits and lime.
2. Pour into a glass over ice and drink immediately.

Super Healthy Juice

Serves 1-2

Ingredients:
- 1 romaine heart
- 5 large carrots
- ½ lemon, peeled
- 2 clementine, peeled
- 1-inch knob of fresh ginger

Directions:
1. Peel the lemon, clementine, and carrots and run through a juicer along with romaine heart, and ginger.
2. For better results, drink this juice once a day.

Blueberry-Cabbage Power Juice

Serves 2

Ingredients:
- 1 cup fresh blueberries
- 1 large cucumber, peeled and cut into chunks
- ¼ medium red cabbage, sliced
- 1 large apple, cut into eighths
- Ice cubes (optional)

Directions:
1. Run the blueberries, cucumber, apple, and cabbage through a juicer.
2. Pour the extracted juice into 2 glasses and enjoy.

Grapefruit Juice with Carrots and Ginger

Serves 1

Ingredients:
- 2 grapefruits, peeled, cut
- 5 carrots, chopped
- 1-inch fresh ginger, peeled and chopped

Directions:
1. Peel the carrots and grapefruit. Pass through a juicer along with the fresh ginger.
2. Pour the juice into a glass, give a stir and drink immediately.

Juice for Weight loss with Grapefruit, Pineapple and Lemon

Serves 1

Ingredients:
- 1 lemon
- ¼ pineapple
- 1 grapefruit
- ½-inch piece of ginger
- ½-inch piece of turmeric

Directions:
1. Wash and peel the fruits. Cut into quarters and place into a juicer along with ginger and turmeric.
2. Drink and get rid of extra pounds.

Sweet and Sour Citrus Juice

Serves 1

Ingredients:

- 2 oranges, peeled
- 1 small or ½ large grapefruit
- 1 to 2 lemons
- ½ inch of turmeric

Directions:

1. Peel the grapefruit, lemon, oranges, and turmeric, cut into quarters, and pass through a juicer.
2. Enjoy.

Apple Almond Juice

Serves 1

Ingredients:
- 1 apple
- ½ orange
- 7-8 almonds, soaked
- ½ sweet potato

Directions:
1. Peel the potato and orange and pass through a juicer along with the almonds and apple.
2. Pour the juice into a glass and enjoy.

Fennel Apple Ginger Juice

Serves 1

Ingredients:
- 1 mango
- 1 apple
- 2 leaves romaine lettuce
- 1 peach
- 1 fennel
- 1 celery stalk
- ½ thumb size piece of ginger

Directions:
1. Run the mango, fennel, apple, peach, celery, and ginger through a juicer.
2. Pour into a glass, stir well and drink immediately.

Tomato Juice

Serves 1

Ingredients:
- 1 cucumber
- 3 cups chopped tomatoes
- 1 stalk celery
- ½ teaspoon of Himalayan Sea salt
- Pinch of pepper
- Pinch of cayenne pepper

Directions:
1. Wash the tomatoes, celery and cucumber, chop and pass through a juicer.
2. Pour the juice into a glass, season with salt, black and cayenne peppers.
3. Stir well and enjoy.

Easy Veggie Juice

Serves 1

Ingredients:
- 1 sweet potato
- 1 beetroot
- 3 medium carrots

Directions:
1. Peel the beetroot, potato and carrots and run through a juicer.
2. Pour into a glass and drink.

Apple Parsnip Carrot Green Juice

Serves 1

Ingredients:
- 3 parsnips
- 3 carrots
- 1 celery stalk
- 1 apple

Directions:
1. Process the carrots, celery, parsnips, and apple through a juicer.
2. Drink immediately.

Healthy Juice Mix

Serves 1

Ingredients:
- 1 golden beetroot
- 3 large carrots
- 4 stalks celery
- ½ cucumber
- ½ thumb of ginger
- 1 medium pear

Directions:
1. Thoroughly wash all ingredients and cut into pieces. Process them through a juicer.
2. Pour the juice into a glass and enjoy.

Daily Detox Juice

Serves 1

Ingredients:
- 1 cup Napa cabbage
- 1 large cucumber
- 1 cup green or red cabbage
- 1 Granny Smith apple
- 4 stalks celery
- 1 cup greens (kale, chard, spinach etc.)
- 4 carrots
- 2 bell peppers (any color)
- 3 red or golden beets (or a combination)
- 1 lemon
- 1 lime
- 1-2-inch piece of ginger root

Directions:
1. Thoroughly wash all the vegetables and cut into chunks.
2. Process through a juicer and drink.

Rainbow Morning Juice

Serves 1

Ingredients:
- 2 carrots
- 2 red peppers
- 1 apple
- 1 broccoli spear

Directions:
1. Thoroughly wash the apple, peppers, carrots, and broccoli and run through a juicer.
2. Ideal to drink in the mornings.

Sweet and Sour Juice

Serves 1

Ingredients:

- 1 mango
- ½ lemon, peeled
- 1 cup blueberries
- 3-4 middle-sized strawberries

Directions:

1. Peel the lemon and put in a juicer followed by the blueberries, mango, and strawberries.
2. Pour the juice into a glass and enjoy.

Pear, Apple Cherry Juice

Serves 1

Ingredients:
- 1 apple
- 1 pear
- ½ cup cherries

Directions:
1. Wash the pear, apple, and cherries, remove the pits, and run through a juicer.
2. Enjoy over ice.

Berry Mix Super Juice

Serves 1

Ingredients:
- 1 cup raspberries
- 1 cup strawberries
- ½ cup blackberries
- 1 cucumber
- ½ cup blueberries

Directions:
1. Wash the berries and cucumber and pass through a juicer.
2. Drink immediately.

Carrot, Ginger and Lime Juice

Serves 2

Ingredients:
- ¼ cup fresh lime juice
- 5 carrots
- 1-4-inch piece ginger

Directions:
1. Pass the carrots, ginger, and lime through a juicer.
2. Pour into a glass and enjoy.

Red Veggie Detox Juice

Serves 1

Ingredients:
- 2 medium beets
- 3 medium tomatoes
- 3 long carrots, cut
- Small piece of ginger

Directions:
1. Wash all the vegetables and pass through a juicer.
2. Pour the juice into a glass and enjoy.

Tomato Carrot, Radish and Juice

Serves 1

Ingredients:
- 15 cherry tomatoes
- 1-2 carrots, peeled
- 2 red radishes, peeled

Directions:
1. Peel the carrots and radishes and add to a juicer along with cherry tomatoes.
2. Pour into a glass and drink immediately.

Detox Radish Fruity Juice

Serves 1

Ingredients:
- 3 celery sticks
- 2 apples
- 2 pears
- 10 radishes

Directions:
1. Wash all ingredients and cut into chunks. Then run through a juicer.
2. Pour the juice into a glass and enjoy.

Radish Carrot Red Juice

Serves 2

Ingredients:
- 2 carrots
- 1 smallish raw beetroot
- 10 French breakfast radishes
- ½ lemon, peeled
- 2 apples

Directions:
1. Wash the carrots, apples, radishes, and beetroot and cut into chunks. Process through a juicer followed by the peeled lemon.
2. Pour the juice into a glass and enjoy.

Carrot, Lime and Ginger Cleanse Juice

Serves 2

Ingredients:
- Small piece ginger
- 2 lbs. (900 g) carrots, peeled
- ¼ cup fresh lime juice

Directions:
1. Wash the carrots and run through a juicer along with a small piece of ginger.
2. Add the lime juice, stir well and drink.

Carrot Tomato Radish Juice

Serves 1

Ingredients:

- 2 long carrots, cut
- 3 medium tomatoes
- 2 red radishes

Directions:

1. Wash the radishes carrots and tomatoes and pass through a juicer.
2. Pour the juice into a glass and drink immediately.

Chapter Two: The Best Green Juice Recipes

Green Citrus Juice

Serves 1

Ingredients:
- 1 lemon
- ¼ cantaloupe
- 1 orange
- Handful of parsley
- Handful of mint

Directions:
1. Peel the lemon, orange and cantaloupe and run through a juicer along with the mint and parsley.
2. Pour the juice into a glass and enjoy.

Green Pineapple

Serves 1

Ingredients:

- 1 small bunch of broccolis (about 2 cups)
- ½ of a pineapple, cut into chunks
- 1 long cucumber, quartered
- 1 kiwi, halved

Directions:

1. Peel the kiwi. Cut the broccoli into florets.
2. Run all the ingredients through a juicer, pour into a tall glass and enjoy immediately. Add ice if desire.

Fennel Apple Mango Green Juice

Serves 1

Ingredients:
- 2 handfuls of spinach
- 2 granny smith apples
- 1 pear, pitted
- 1 fennel
- 1 mango
- 1 celery stalk
- ½ thumb size piece of ginger

Directions:
1. Wash all ingredients and process through a juicer.
2. Pour the extracted juice into a glass, stir well and drink immediately.

Light Green Juice

Serves 1

Ingredients:
- 2 apples
- 1 bunch spinach
- ½ lemon, peeled

Directions:
1. Wash the spinach, apples and lemon and cut into chunks.
2. Add to a juicer and process.
3. Pour into a glass and drink immediately.

Citrus Veggie Green Juice

Serves 1

Ingredients:
- 1 medium beet, peeled
- 2 leaves of red cabbage
- 3 medium carrots
- ½ lemon, peeled
- 1 orange, peeled
- ½ pineapple
- 2 handfuls of spinach

Directions:
1. Peel the pineapple, beet, orange and citrus and process through a juicer along with spinach, carrots, and cabbage leaves.
2. Pour the extracted juice into a glass and enjoy.

Green Juice

Serves 1

Ingredients:
- 2 stalks of celery
- ½ lemon
- ½ bunch of kale
- 3-inch chunk of daikon radish
- 1 small cucumber
- ½ bunch of spinach
- A few sprigs of cilantro or flat leaf parsley

Directions:
1. Pass the celery, kale, radish, cucumber, spinach, lemon, and cilantro through a juicer.
2. If the juice is too strong for you, add a pear or apple to sweeten it.

Pineapple Miracle

Serves 1

Ingredients:
- ½ pineapple
- 1 bunch parsley
- A handful of mint leaves

Directions:
1. Process the parsley, mint, and pineapple through a juicer.
2. Pour into a glass over ice and enjoy.
3. You may experience this juice adding some kale, spinach, or collards.

Quick and Easy Green Juice with Celery, Kale and Lemon

Serves 1

Ingredients:
- 1 bunch kale
- 1 bunch celery
- 1 lemon

Directions:
1. Wash the celery kale and lemon and run through a juicer.
2. Drink immediately.

Super Healthy Green Juice

Serves 1

Ingredients:
- 2 cups Swiss chard
- 1 cup kale
- 2 carrots
- 2 celery stalks
- 2 apples

Directions:
1. Add the greens to a juicer and process along with apples, carrots, and celery stalks.
2. Pour the juice into a glass and drink immediately.

Green Cabbage Juice

Serves 1

Ingredients:
- ½ head green or Napa cabbage
- 1 bunch dandelion greens
- ½ bunch celery
- ½ lemon, unpeeled
- 1-inch knob of fresh ginger root

Directions:
1. Process the cabbage, celery, dandelion greens, lemon, and ginger through a juicer.
2. Add little honey to provide the juice some sweetness.

Super Cleanse Juice

Serves 1

Ingredients:

- 1 bunch celery
- ½ head purple cabbage
- 1 lemon

Directions:

1. Process the celery, purple cabbage, and lemon through a juicer.
2. Pour into a glass over ice and enjoy.

Green Power Juice

Serves 1

Ingredients:
- 2 stalks celery
- 2 small apples
- 2 carrots
- 5 small radishes
- 1 small piece ginger
- 1 cup spinach

Directions:
1. Wash the apples, carrots, radishes, spinach and cut into chunks.
2. Add to a juicer along with a piece of ginger.
3. Pour the extracted juice into a glass, stir well and drink.

Super Effective Green Juice with Pineapple and Herbs

Serves 1

Ingredients:
- 2 leaves Swiss chard
- 1 cup kale
- ½ cup parsley
- ½ small beet
- ½ cup pineapple, chipped
- 2 medium green apples, chopped
- 1 sprig fresh mint
- ½ medium lemon, peeled

Directions:
1. Wash the herbs under running water. Make sure not to leave dirt on the leaves. Place in a juicer.
2. Add the beet, pineapple, green apples and lemon and process.
3. Pour into a tall glass and enjoy.

Beach Babe Juice Recipe for Weight Loss

Serves 1-2

Ingredients:

- 1 cucumber
- 1 head romaine lettuce
- 1 lemon, peeled
- 1 lime, peeled
- 1 orange, peeled
- 2 apples
- 1 pint of berries (blackberries, raspberries)
- 4 large carrots

Directions:

1. Run the cucumber, lime, lemon, orange, carrots, apples, berries, and lettuce through a juicer.
2. Pour into a glass and enjoy.
3. For better results, drink the juice in the morning.

Green Juice for Cleanse

Serves 1

Ingredients:
- 2 leaves Swiss chard
- 2 leaves collard greens
- 1 cup kale
- 1 cup spinach
- ½ medium cucumber
- 1-inch fresh ginger root, peeled
- ½ medium lemon, peeled

Directions:
1. Wash the greens under running water.
2. Remove the lemon rind.
3. Run all the produce through a juicer, pour into a glass and enjoy immediately.

Fat Burning Juice Recipe

Serves 1

Ingredients:
- 1 pink grapefruit, peeled
- 2 oranges, peeled
- 1 bunch mint
- 1 head romaine lettuce

Directions:
1. Peel the oranges and grapefruit.
2. Pass the citruses through a juicer along with mint and lettuce and enjoy.

Green Detox Juice for Weight Loss

Serves 1

Ingredients:
- 1 green apple
- 1 cucumber
- 2 handfuls of spinach
- 1 handful of parsley
- 1 celery stick

Directions:
1. Pass the cucumber along with spinach, parsley, celery, and apple through a juicer.
2. Pour into a glass over ice and serve immediately.

Belly Buster Green Juice Recipe

Serves 1

Ingredients:
- 3 medium apples
- 3 small mandarins, skin on
- 1 large cucumber
- 1 lime, skin on
- 1 large lemon, skin on
- 1 head romaine lettuce

Directions:
1. Thoroughly wash the vegetables and fruits as we are going to use them unpeeled.
2. Then run all ingredients through a juicer.
3. Enjoy immediately.

Pineapple Green Juice

Serves 1

Ingredients:

- 1 Granny Smith apple
- 1 cup pineapple
- 1 large broccoli stalk and florets
- 5 kale leaves
- 1 cup spinach, torn
- Big handful of fresh mint

Directions:

1. Cut the broccoli into florets and pass through a juicer along with chopped pineapple, apple, kale, spinach, and mint.
2. Pour into a tall glass over ice and enjoy.

Fat Burning Juice with Asparagus, Apples and Cucumber

Serves 1

Ingredients:
- 1 or 2 asparagus stalks
- 1 medium cucumber
- 1 cup spinach leaves
- 3 celery stalks or ribs
- ½ ripe tomato
- 2 apples, quartered

Directions:
1. Thoroughly wash the greens making sure not to leave dirt on leaves.
2. Wash the apples, tomato and cucumber and cut into quarters.
3. Pass all the ingredients through a juicer and drink immediately.

Tasty Green Juice for Weight Loss

Serves 1

Ingredients:

- 1 lime, unpeeled
- 2 cups spinach
- 8 large kale leaves
- 12 strawberries
- 2 Granny Smith apples
- A handful of fresh mint

Directions:

1. Thoroughly wash the kale, spinach, lime, apples, mint, and strawberries.
2. Run all the ingredients through a juicer.
3. Pour the extracted juice into a tall glass over ice and drink immediately.

Pineapple Apple Kale Juice

Serves 1

Ingredients:
- ½ large cucumber
- 6-8 large leaves of kale with stem
- ½ bunch parsley or cilantro
- ⅓ pineapple flesh, peeled
- 1 medium yellow or green apple

Directions:
1. Wash the kale, cucumber, parsley, and apple. Remove the skin from the pineapple.
2. Run all the ingredients through a juicer and drink immediately.

Carrot Apple Spinach Juice

Serves 1-2

Ingredients:
- 4-5 carrots
- 2 apples
- 2 cups spinach

Directions:
1. Wash the carrots, apples, and spinach under running water.
2. Cut into chunks and pass through a juicer.
3. Enjoy immediately.

Watercress and Carrot Juice

Serves 1

Ingredients:

- ½ cup spinach, torn
- 1 cup watercress, chopped
- 2-3 medium sized carrots
- 2 Roma tomatoes, diced
- ½ cup cilantro, roughly chopped
- ½ tsp ground black pepper
- ½ tsp kosher salt

Directions:

1. Wash the carrots and tomatoes and cut into chunks. Run through a juicer along with spinach, watercress, and cilantro.
2. Pour the juice into a tall glass. Add the kosher salt and black pepper, stir well and drink immediately.

Green Juice

Serves 2

Ingredients:
- 2 green apples, halved
- 4 stalks celery
- 1 cucumber, pealed
- 6 romaine leaves
- 5 kale leaves
- 1 lemon, peeled

Directions:
1. Thoroughly wash all the ingredients under running cold water and run the through a juicer.
2. Pour the juice into 2 glasses and serve with ice.

Green Juice for Beginners

Serves 2

Ingredients
- 1 lime
- 4 kale leaves
- 1/3 pineapple
- 2 red apples
- 1-inch knob of ginger
- A handful Italian parsley

Directions:
1. Wash the kale, parsley, lime, and apples. Remove the zest of the lime. Cut the apples into chunks and run through a juicer, alternating with the remaining ingredients.
2. Apples will ease the process by pushing down the other ingredients.
3. Pour the fresh juice into a tall glass and drink immediately.

Rich Green Juice

Serves 1

Ingredients:

- 1-2 stalks celery
- 1 green apple, seeds removed
- 1 large orange, peeled
- 1 small bunch organic kale
- 2 small handfuls spinach
- 1-inch piece of fresh ginger
- 1 large carrot
- Freshly squeezed lemon juice to taste

Directions:

1. Thoroughly wash the fruits and vegetables.
2. Run through a juicer and pour into a tall glass.
3. Stir in the freshly squeezed lemon juice to your taste, add 2-3 ice cubes and enjoy.

Belly Fat Busting Juice Recipe

Serves 1

Ingredients:
- 1 red pepper
- 1 large handful of spinach, torn
- 1 medium cucumber, halved
- 3 medium carrots

Directions:
1. Wash the spinach, cucumber, carrots, and red pepper.
2. Run through a juicer. Pour the extracted juice into a glass and drink immediately.

Easy Green Juice Recipe for Weight Loss

Serves 1

Ingredients:
- 3 large kale leaves
- 2 handfuls of spinach
- 1 cucumber, quartered
- 2 cups fresh berries (strawberries and blackberries)

Directions:
1. Wash all the ingredients.
2. Run the spinach and kale through a juicer followed by cucumber and berries.
3. Pour the extracted juice into a tall glass and drink immediately.

Tomato Basil Cleanse Juicing Recipe

Serves 1

Ingredients:
- 5 tomatoes
- 1 cup of basil
- 2 handfuls of spinach
- ½ cucumber, unpeeled

Directions:
1. Wash all the produce under running water.
2. Run the spinach and basil through a juicer followed by tomatoes and cucumber.
3. Pour the juice into a tall glass and enjoy.

Tasty and Healthy Green Juicing Recipe for Weight Loss

Serves 1

Ingredients:

- 1 green apple, cut into quarters
- ½ lime
- 1 medium cucumber
- 2 handfuls of kale, chopped
- ¼ cup raspberries

Directions:

1. Run the cucumber, apple, lime, kale, and raspberries through a juicer.
2. Pour the extracted juice into a glass and drink immediately.

Apple Mint Energizing Booster Juice Recipe

Serves 1

Ingredients:
- 5 apples, cored
- 5-6 springs of mint (or to taste)

Directions:
1. Wash the apples, core, and cut into quarters.
2. Pass through a juicer along with fresh mint.
3. Pour the juice into a glass and drink immediately.

Pineapple Cucumber Mint Juice

Serves 1

Ingredients:
- 2 cucumbers
- ½ ripe pineapple
- 1 bunch of mint

Directions:
1. Pass the cucumbers, pineapple, and mint through a juicer.
2. Pour into a tall glass and drink immediately.

Kale Orange Apple Green Juice

Serves 2

Ingredients:
- 1 medium orange, peeled
- 3 kale leaves
- 1 medium apple, cut into wedges

Directions:
1. Peel and cut the apple and orange. Add to a juicer along with kale leaves.
2. Pour the extracted juice into a glass and enjoy.

Apple and Pear Mint Juice

Serves 2

Ingredients:

- 1 cucumber
- 4 red apples
- 4 pears
- 1 cup of fresh mint leaves

Directions:

1. Wash the pears, apples, cucumber, and mint leaves.
2. Run all ingredients through a juicer and drink immediately.

Kale Celery Fruity Juice

Serves 1

Ingredients:
- 3 leaves kale
- 2 red plums
- 3 stalks celery
- 1 apple

Directions:
1. Pit the plums and core the apples. Add to a juicer along with kale and celery.
2. Process and enjoy.

Healthy Green Juice

Serves 1-2

Ingredients:

- 2 green apples, halved
- 4 stalks celery, leaves removed
- 1 cucumber
- 6 leaves kale
- ½ lemon, peeled
- 1 (1-inch) piece fresh ginger

Directions:

1. Thoroughly wash all ingredients, cut, and run through a juicer.
2. Pour into a juicer and enjoy.

Healthy Morning Juice

Serves 2

Ingredients:

- 3 medium carrots, in chunks
- 2-3 leaves kale, roughly sliced
- 3 stalks celery, roughly chopped
- 2-3 medium apples, cut in chunks

Directions:

1. Wash the kale, celery, apples, and carrots.
2. Run through a juicer and pour into two glasses.
3. Add 1-2 ice cubes (if desire) and enjoy.

Savory Green Juice

Serves 1

Ingredients:
- 4-5 kale leaves
- 1 lime
- 1 green apple
- 1 big handful of flat leaf parsley leaves
- 1 lemon
- 1 bunch celery
- 1-inch of fresh ginger
- 1 tablespoon coconut oil

Directions:
1. Wash the herbs and peel the lime, lemon, and ginger.
2. Run all ingredients through a juicer. Pour the extracted juice into a glass and drink immediately.

Kale Lettuce Detox Juice

Serves 1

Ingredients:

- ½ medium cucumber
- 2 medium stalks celery
- 4 romaine heart leaves or 2 outer leaves
- 2 kale leaves
- 1 cup spinach
- 1 medium green apple
- 1 lemon, rind and pith removed
- 1 slice ginger

Directions:

1. Thoroughly wash all ingredients and pass through a juicer.
2. Pour the juice into a glass and enjoy.

Green Apple Kiwi and Kale Juice

Serves 2-3

Ingredients:
- 2 green apples
- 1 bunch kale, stemmed
- 2 kiwis, peeled
- 1 heart of romaine lettuce
- 1 cucumber
- Juice of 1 lemon

Directions:
1. Rinse the kiwis, apples, romaine, kale, and cucumber. Peel the kiwi and run through a juicer followed by the apples, kale, cucumber, and lettuce.
2. Finally stir in the lemon juice and drink immediately.

Carrot Orange Kale Green Juice

Serves 1

Ingredients:
- 2 big handfuls of kale
- 2 oranges
- 4 carrots
- ½ a lemon
- A knob of ginger about an inch long

Directions:
1. Peel the oranges and pass through a juicer along with carrots, kale, lemon, and ginger.
2. Pour into a glass and enjoy.

Celery Pear Healthy Green Juice

Serves 1

Ingredients:
- 2 stalks celery
- 6 pears
- 3 cups kale
- 2 tablespoons fresh mint

Directions:
1. Quarter the pears and remove the seeds. Pass through a juicer along with celery, kale, and mint.
2. Pour the juice into a glass and drink.

Green Veggie Juice

Serves 1

Ingredients:

- 2 radishes
- ½ head cauliflower
- 13 Brussels sprouts
- ¼ head green cabbage

Directions:

1. Wash the cauliflower and cut into florets and pass through a juicer. Wash the remaining ingredients and add to the juicer.
2. Pour the juice into a glass, stir well and drink immediately.

Green Paradise

Serves 1

Ingredients:
- 1 pear
- 4 stalks celery
- 2 stalks kale
- 1 cup spinach
- ½ lemon juice

Directions:
1. Wash the greens, pear and lemon and cut into chunks. Then pass all ingredients through a juicer.
2. Pour into a glass and drink immediately.

Green Dream

Serves 1

Ingredients:
- 3 stalks celery
- 2/3 cucumber
- 1 cup broccoli
- 2 green apples
- ½ lemon

Directions:
1. Wash the celery, cucumber, broccoli, apples, and lemon and run through a juicer.
2. Pour the juice into a glass, stir well, and enjoy.

Green Royal Juice

Serves 1

Ingredients:
- ½ head broccoli
- 4 leaves kale
- ½ green bell pepper
- 1 zucchini, peeled
- 1 green apple

Directions:
1. Wash the pepper, broccoli, zucchini, kale, and apple and cut into chunks.
2. Then pass all ingredients through a juicer.
3. Pour the juice into a glass and drink immediately.

Conclusion

We hope you enjoy the cookbook and that we have introduced a wild splash of energy through healthy, revitalizing and amazingly tasty juicing recipes, carefully selected and nicely presented in it. You are offered a large choice of vegetable, fruit, berry, and herbal juices, all of which are rich in vitamins, phytonutrients, soluble fiber, and microelements, which are extremely important for keeping fit, energetic, and healthy. The book was aimed at helping you discover as many interesting combinations of various juices as possible so that your everyday juicing procedure is not restrained to just apples, carrots, or strawberries. While having this book at hand, you definitely won't miss out on green leafy vegetables, such as spinach, broccoli, arugula, collard greens, wheatgrass, lettuce, etc., as well as such important fruits, such as starfruit, papaya, grapefruit, dragon fruits, avocado, etc., that are often absent in the contemporary diet and slapdash lifestyle.

These recipes are sure to make a major change in your life, which you will notice from the very first week of starting your exciting adventure into the world on juicing. However, we strongly recommend that you follow the ingredient lists closely and not overdo with your daily intake of juices because a small cup of freshly squeezed juice may contain more calories than a whole meal. Therefore, you need to make sure you are ready to embark on an active lifestyle and make the best use of these healthy calories, using them for energy and not for a fat layer around the waistline.

Here is when talking needs to be replaced by action! So, hurry up and juice something right now.

Finally, if you enjoyed this book, please take the time to share your thoughts and post a review on Amazon. It would be greatly appreciated!

Thank you and good luck!

Made in the USA
Columbia, SC
26 September 2024